Clear Mind Clear Choices

Las Redan

Published by Las Redan, 2024.

CLEAR MIND CLEAR CHOICES

First edition. September 23, 2024.

ISBN: 979-8227070203

Written by Las Redan.

Table of Contents

Preface

In our fast-paced, information-saturated world, the choices we make every day can feel overwhelming. From the mundane decisions about what to eat for breakfast to the significant crossroads that shape our careers and relationships, each choice is influenced by a myriad of factors, many of which operate beneath the surface of our consciousness. Among these factors, our biases—often unrecognized and unexamined—can significantly distort our perception of reality and impact our decision-making processes. "Clear Mind, Clear Choices" was born out of a desire to illuminate this often-overlooked aspect of our lives. The journey toward understanding our biases is not merely an intellectual exercise; it is a transformative process that can lead to greater clarity, empathy, and authenticity in our choices. This book combines the ancient wisdom of mindfulness practices with

contemporary insights from psychology and neuroscience, creating a roadmap to help you navigate your biases and make more conscious choices. Throughout these pages, you will find a blend of research findings, practical exercises, and personal anecdotes designed to guide you in cultivating mindfulness and self-awareness. The goal is not to eliminate biases entirely—after all, they are an intrinsic part of the human experience

—but to recognize and understand them so that they no longer dictate our actions in unconscious ways. As you embark on this journey, I encourage you to approach the material with an open mind and a willingness to engage in self-reflection. Each chapter invites you to explore new perspectives and to challenge the assumptions you may hold about yourself and the world around you.

By practicing mindfulness, you will develop the ability to pause, re ect, and choose intentionally, allowing you to break free from the automatic patterns that may have previously guided your decisions. This book is for anyone seeking to lead a more intentional and fulfilling life, whether you are a seasoned practitioner of mindfulness or just beginning to explore its potential.

Together, let us embrace the journey toward a clearer mind and clearer choices, transforming our understanding of ourselves and the world in the process. Welcome to "Clear Mind, Clear Choices." May it serve as a beacon of insight and empowerment on your path to greater awareness and decision-making.

Chapter 1: Understanding the Mind

- The Power of the Mind
- How Biases Shape Our Decisions
- The Role of Mindfulness in Clarity

The Power of the Mind

The mind is a powerful tool, capable of shaping our perceptions, decisions, and ultimately, our lives. When we harness the power of our minds through mindfulness, we create a space for clarity and understanding. This clarity allows us to see beyond the fog of cognitive biases that often cloud our judgment. By practicing mindfulness, we can train ourselves to become more aware of our thoughts and feelings, enabling us to distinguish between what is truly important and what is merely a distraction. This journey begins with a simple yet profound realization: the mind has the capacity to change.

The power of the mind is a profound and multifaceted concept that encompasses various aspects of human experience, including thought, perception, emotion, and intention. The mind has the ability to shape reality through beliefs and attitudes, influencing both individual lives and broader societal outcomes. At a personal level, the mind can drive motivation and determination. Positive thinking and visualization techniques can enhance performance in various fields, from sports to business. The placebo effect illustrates how belief in a treatment can lead to real physiological changes, highlighting the mind's capacity to affect the body.

Moreover, the power of the mind extends to emotional regulation. Techniques such as meditation and mindfulness can help individuals manage stress, anxiety, and depression, fostering a greater sense of well-being. These practices enhance self-awareness and promote a clearer understanding of one's thoughts and feelings, allowing for healthier responses to life's challenges. On a collective scale, the mind can influence social dynamics and cultural shifts. Collective beliefs and shared visions can inspire movements for change, demonstrating how a unified mindset can lead to significant societal transformations. History is replete with examples where the power of collective thought has sparked revolutions or advancements in science and art. Additionally, the mind's creative potential is limitless. It fosters imagination, enabling individuals to conceive innovative ideas and solutions. This creativity fuels progress in technology, literature, and the arts, contributing to the rich tapestry of human achievement.

In summary, the power of the mind is a central force in shaping experiences, fostering resilience, and driving innovation. Its influence is evident in personal growth, emotional health, and societal change, underscoring the importance of nurturing and harnessing this incredible capability.

Mindfulness invites us to observe our thoughts without judgment, creating a foundation for better decision-making. When we approach our thoughts with curiosity rather than criticism, we can identify patterns that lead to biased thinking. For example, the tendency to favor information that confirms our existing beliefs can limit our understanding and hinder our choices. By practicing mindfulness, we can recognize these patterns and consciously choose to seek out diverse perspectives. This shift in awareness empowers us to break free from the confines of our biases and make choices that reflect our true values and goals.

One effective strategy for overcoming cognitive biases is to cultivate a habit of reflective thinking. Setting aside time each day to reflect on our decisions can illuminate the thought processes that underlie them. During this time, we can ask ourselves questions like, "What influenced my decision?" or "Am I considering all available options?" Such reaction encourages a deeper understanding of our motivations and concerns, fostering a sense of confidence in our ability to navigate complex choices. As we become more attuned to our thought patterns, we gain the tools to challenge our biases and approach decision-making with a clearer mind.

In addition to reactive thinking, mindfulness practices such as meditation can further enhance our mental clarity. By dedicating just a few minutes each day to quiet our minds, we create a sanctuary of peace that allows our thoughts to settle. This practice not only reduces stress but also sharpens our focus, making it easier to engage in the decision-making process with a calm and clear mindset. As we learn to quiet the noise in our minds, we can access deeper insights and make choices that align more closely with our true desires and intentions.

Ultimately, the power of the mind lies in its ability to transform our experiences and choices. By embracing mindfulness, we unlock the potential to overcome biases that have held us back and foster a con dent approach to decision-making. Each moment spent practicing mindfulness is a step toward cultivating a clearer mind and making choices that resonate with our authentic selves. As we embark on this journey, we must remember that every small effort contributes to a larger transformation, empowering us to lead lives led with intention and purpose.

How Biases Shape Our Decisions

Biases are an inherent part of the human experience, affecting our decisions in ways we often fail to recognize. From the moment we wake up to when we go to sleep, our minds are bombarded with information that we must alter through our personal beliefs, experiences, and emotions. These biases can lead us to make choices that are less than optimal, often steering us away from what we truly want or need. By understanding how biases operate, we can begin to untangle the web of in nuances that shape our daily decisions, ultimately leading to a clearer, more con dent path forward.

The good news is that mindfulness can serve as a powerful tool in combatting these biases. When we practice mindfulness, we cultivate an awareness of our thoughts and feelings, allowing us to step back and observe our decision-making processes without immediate judgment. This heightened awareness creates space for reflection, enabling us to identify when biases are influencing our choices.

To begin this journey, consider employing simple mindfulness strategies that encourage clarity of thought. Start by incorporating moments of pause into your daily routine—whether through deep breathing exercises or brief meditative practices. During these moments, focus on observing your thoughts without attachment. Acknowledge the biases that arise and remind yourself that they do not de ne your reality. By developing this habit, you can gradually enhance your ability to make decisions grounded in awareness rather than automatic reactions.

Another effective approach is to seek out diverse perspectives when faced with a decision. Engaging with others who hold different viewpoints can shine a light on the biases that may have clouded your judgment. This practice not only broadens your understanding but also fosters a sense of community and support. When you open yourself up to alternative ideas, you cultivate a richer decision-making process that is informed by a variety of experiences rather than solely your own.

Ultimately, embracing mindfulness and actively working to overcome biases is a journey of growth and self-discovery. As you become more attuned to how these biases shape your decisions, you will gain the confidence and motivation to make choices that reflect your authentic self. Remember, every small step you take toward mindfulness and clarity is a victory. With patience and persistence, you will find that your decision- making skills improve, paving the way for a more fulfilling and intentional life.

The Role of Mindfulness in Clarity

Mindfulness plays a crucial role in enhancing clarity of thought, particularly for those who often find themselves overwhelmed by choices and uncertainties. By focusing on the present moment, mindfulness allows individuals to step back from the noise of their thoughts and emotions. This practice creates a mental space that enables clearer thinking, making it easier to analyze situations without the cloud of biases. This awareness is the first step toward making more informed decisions.

One of the most significant impacts of mindfulness is its ability to reduce stress and anxiety, which are often barriers to clarity. When our minds are cluttered with worry about the future or regret about the past, it becomes difficult to see the present accurately. Mindfulness encourages you to acknowledge these feelings without judgment, allowing them to come and go rather than letting them dominate your thoughts. As you practice being present, you'll find that your ability to think clearly improves, enabling you to approach decisions with a fresh perspective and a calm mind.

To harness the power of mindfulness for clearer decision-making, consider integrating simple strategies into your daily routine. Start with short, focused breathing exercises that ground you in the moment. Even just a few minutes of deep breathing can clear your mind of distractions, providing the clarity needed to assess your options.

Another effective strategy is to practice mindfulness in your decision- making process. When faced with a choice, take a moment to pause and breathe deeply before reacting. This pause allows you to gather your thoughts and assess the situation without the immediate influence of emotional or cognitive biases. By incorporating this mindful approach, you empower yourself to weigh the pros and cons more objectively, leading to decisions that align more closely with your true values and goals.

Ultimately, the journey to clarity through mindfulness is about progress, not perfection. Embracing this practice may feel challenging at first, but with patience and dedication, you will notice a shift in how you approach decisions. As you cultivate mindfulness, you will not only enhance your clarity of thought but also build the confidence and motivation necessary to navigate life's choices with ease. Remember, every small step counts, and with each mindful moment, you are moving closer to a clearer, more empowered version of yourself.

Chapter 2: The Basics of Mindfulness

- What is Mindfulness?
- Benefits of Mindfulness for Everyday Life
- Simple Mindfulness Practices to Get Started

What is Mindfulness?

Mindfulness is the practice of being fully present in the moment, allowing you to engage with your thoughts, feelings, and surroundings without judgment. It encourages a state of awareness where distractions and anxieties fade into the background, creating space for clarity and insight. For everyday individuals who often feel overwhelmed by choices or uncertain about their decisions, embracing mindfulness can pave the way for more con dent and informed actions. By anchoring yourself in the present, you begin to notice patterns in your thinking that may have previously gone unnoticed.

At its core, mindfulness teaches you to observe your thoughts and emotions as they arise, rather than reacting impulsively. This observation creates a mental distance from your automatic responses, empowering you to respond thoughtfully instead of reflexively. Many people struggle with cognitive biases—systematic patterns of deviation from norm or rationality in judgment—that cloud their decision-making process. Mindfulness equips with the tools to recognize these biases, allowing you to pause and reflect before making choices that might be influenced by preconceived notions or emotional triggers.

One effective strategy to cultivate mindfulness is through meditation. Even just a few minutes of focused breathing can enhance your awareness and help ground your thoughts. As you practice, you may notice how often your mind drifts toward worries or regrets, leading to a clouded judgment. By acknowledging these thoughts without judgment, you create an opportunity to redirect your focus toward what truly matters, ultimately leading to clearer choices. This simple yet powerful practice can transform your approach to daily decisions, making you more adept at navigating life's complexities.

Incorporating mindfulness into your daily routine can also enhance your confidence and motivation. By regularly taking time to check in with yourself and your feelings, you can better understand your values and priorities, which serve as a compass for decision-making. As you become more attuned to your inner voice, you may find that your self-doubt diminishes. Confidence is built through consistent practice, and mindfulness can help you cultivate a resilient mindset that embraces challenges rather than shying away from them.

The journey to harnessing mindfulness is not about achieving perfection but rather about embracing progress. Each moment spent practicing mindfulness is a step toward greater clarity and understanding. As you learn to navigate your thoughts and feelings with compassion and awareness, you will uncover the potential to overcome biases and make choices that resonate with your true self. Remember, every moment you choose to practice mindfulness is an investment in your growth and empowerment, leading to a more fulfilling and intentional life.

Benefits of Mindfulness for Everyday Life

Mindfulness offers a powerful toolkit for enhancing clarity of thought, which is essential for making informed decisions in everyday life. By cultivating present-moment awareness, individuals can better observe their thoughts and feelings without judgment.

This practice allows for a clearer understanding of one's internal landscape, which is often clouded by distractions, worries, and preconceived notions. When you embrace mindfulness, you gain the ability to sift through the chaos of daily life and identify what truly matters, leading to more thoughtful and deliberate choices.

Incorporating mindfulness into your daily routine can significantly boost your confidence. When you are attuned to your thoughts and emotions, you become more aware of the biases that may influence your decision-making. This awareness acts as a shield against self-doubt and negative self-talk, empowering you to approach challenges with a more positive mindset. As you practice mindfulness, you will find that your capacity to trust your instincts and make choices based on clarity rather than fear will grow, fostering a sense of confidence in your abilities.

Mindfulness also serves as an effective strategy for overcoming cognitive biases that can cloud judgment. Many people are unaware of the mental shortcuts they take, which often lead to poor decisions. By practicing mindfulness, you can recognize these biases as they arise and pause before reacting. This pause allows for deeper reflection and a chance to consider alternative perspectives. Over time, this practice not only helps to reduce the influence of biases but also encourages a more open-minded approach to problem-solving, enabling you to see situations from multiple angles and make better-informed choices.

In addition to improving decision-making, mindfulness enhances motivation by fostering a sense of purpose and engagement in daily activities. When you are fully present, you can appreciate the small joys in life, which can reignite your passion for tasks that may have previously felt mundane. This renewed engagement can lead to increased productivity and a greater willingness to tackle challenges.

As you cultivate mindfulness, you may find that your motivation naturally rises, allowing you to pursue your goals with vigor and enthusiasm.

Ultimately, the benefits of mindfulness extend into every facet of life, transforming not just the way you make decisions, but also how you experience the world around you. By fostering clarity of thought, boosting confidence, and enhancing motivation, mindfulness empowers you to navigate the complexities of everyday life with grace and ease.

Simple Mindfulness Practices

Simple Mindfulness Practices to Get Started Mindfulness is a powerful tool that can transform the way you think and make decisions. Simple mindfulness practices can help you cultivate a clear mind, allowing you to navigate everyday choices with greater confidence and clarity. Starting a mindfulness practice doesn't require a lot of time or special equipment; it can be integrated into your daily routine in small, manageable ways. By committing to these practices, you can begin to overcome cognitive biases that cloud your judgment and hinder your decision-making abilities.

One of the simplest ways to practice mindfulness is through focused breathing. Take a few moments each day to sit quietly and pay attention to your breath. Inhale deeply through your nose, allowing your abdomen to expand, and then exhale slowly through your mouth. As you breathe, direct your attention solely to the sensation of your breath entering and leaving your body. If your mind wanders, gently redirect your focus back to your breathing. This practice not only calms your mind but also enhances your ability to concentrate, helping you to think more clearly about the choices you face.

Another effective mindfulness exercise is the practice of gratitude. Each day, take a moment to reflect on three things you are grateful for. This could be anything from a warm cup of coffee to a kind word from a friend. By intentionally focusing on the positive aspects of your life, you shift your mindset from negativity and bias toward a more balanced perspective. This shift can significantly impact your decision-making process, enabling you to approach choices with a sense of appreciation rather than fear or doubt.

Mindful observation is another valuable practice. Choose an object in your environment—a plant, a piece of art, or even a simple object like a pen— and observe it closely for a few minutes. Notice its colors, textures, and any other details that stand out to you. This practice encourages you to slow down and engage your senses, fostering a greater awareness of the present moment. By honing your observational skills, you can develop a clearer understanding of your thoughts and feelings, allowing you to make decisions that align better with your true self.

Mindfulness is valuable because it enhances self-awareness, allowing individuals to better understand their thoughts and emotions. This increased awareness can lead to improved emotional regulation and reduced stress levels. Mindfulness practices promote relaxation and can help decrease symptoms of anxiety and depression. Additionally, being present in the moment fosters a greater appreciation for life and can improve relationships by encouraging better communication and empathy. It also supports mental clarity and focus, which can enhance productivity and decision-making. Overall, mindfulness contributes to overall well-being and a healthier, more balanced lifestyle.

Finally, incorporating mindful walking into your routine can be a refreshing way to enhance your mindfulness practice. Whether you take a stroll in your neighborhood or walk in a park, pay attention to the sensations in your body as you move. Feel the ground beneath your feet, notice the rhythm of your steps, and observe your surroundings. This practice not only clears your mind but also encourages a sense of connection to the world around you. As you become more attuned to your environment, you will find it easier to approach decisions with a level-headed mindset, free from the distractions of cognitive biases. By integrating these simple practices into your life, you can build a strong foundation for clearer thinking and more con dent decision-making.

Chapter 3: Recognizing Your Biases

- Common Cognitive Biases
- Self-Reflection: Identifying Your Own Biases
- The Importance of Awareness

Common Cognitive biases

Cognitive biases are systematic patterns of deviation from norm or rationality in judgment, and they can significant affect our decision- making processes. These biases often lead us to make choices based on awed reasoning rather than objective analysis. One common bias is confirmation bias, where individuals favor information that supports their existing beliefs while ignoring evidence that contradicts them. Recognizing this bias is the first step toward making clearer, more informed decisions. By practicing mindfulness, you can learn to observe your thoughts and feelings without judgment, allowing you to identify when confirmation bias is influencing your choices.

Another prevalent bias is the availability heuristic, which occurs when people overestimate the importance of information that is readily available to them. For example, if you frequently hear news stories about plane crashes, you might overestimate the danger of flying, despite it being one of the safest modes of transportation. Mindfulness can help you step back from these emotional reactions and assess situations more rationally. By cultivating a practice of present-moment awareness, you can train your mind to consider a broader range of information before making decisions, leading to more balanced outcomes.

Anchoring is yet another cognitive bias that impacts our choices. This occurs when an initial piece of information sets a standard for future judgments, often leading us to make decisions based on arbitrary references. For instance, the rst price you see for a product might anchor your perception of its value, affecting how you perceive subsequent prices. Mindfulness can encourage you to question these anchors by fostering a sense of curiosity and openness. This can empower you to explore options without being unduly influenced by initial information, allowing for healthier decision-making.

Overconfidence bias is a common pitfall as well, where individuals overestimate their knowledge or predictive abilities. This can lead to poor choices based on inflated self-assessments. Practicing mindfulness can ground you in reality, helping you acknowledge your limitations and encouraging a humbler approach to decision-making. By being present and aware of your thought patterns, you can cultivate a sense of realism that enhances your confidence while also recognizing when you might need to seek additional information or support.

Incorporating mindfulness into your daily routine can profoundly impact your ability to recognize and counteract these cognitive biases. As you develop a clearer understanding of how these biases operate, you empower yourself to make decisions that reflect your true values and goals. Every small step you take towards mindfulness can lead to greater clarity of thought, improved decision-making skills, and increased confidence in your choices. Embracing this journey not only helps you overcome biases but also fosters a more fulfilling and intentional life.

Self-Reflection: Identifying Your Own Biases

Self-refection is an essential tool in the journey toward greater clarity and decision-making prowess. Every individual carries a unique set of biases formed by personal experiences, societal influences, and cultural backgrounds. These biases often operate unconsciously, shaping our perceptions and judgments without us realizing it. By taking the time to engage in self-reflection, you can begin to uncover these hidden biases, creating a clearer path to more informed choices.

To embark on this journey of self-discovery, start by creating a quiet space for yourself. This can be a cozy corner in your home or a peaceful spot in nature where distractions are minimal. Sit comfortably, breathe deeply, and allow your mind to settle. As thoughts arise, observe them without judgment. What beliefs or assumptions come to the forefront? Are there recurring themes in your thoughts about certain groups of people or situations? This awareness is the first step in identifying where biases may exist in your mindset.

Once you have noticed these biases, it's important to explore their origins. Ask yourself where these beliefs came from. Did they stem from personal experiences, societal narratives, or cultural teachings? Understanding the roots of your biases helps you realize that they are not immutable truths but rather constructs that can be challenged and changed. This realization can be empowering, as it gives you the opportunity to redefine your perspectives and open your mind to new possibilities.

Another effective strategy is to engage in conversations with others who hold different viewpoints. Listening to diverse perspectives can challenge your existing beliefs and encourage you to think critically about your biases. Approach these discussions with curiosity rather than defensiveness. This open-mindedness not only fosters a deeper understanding of others but also allows you to reflect on how your biases might color your interpretation of their experiences.

Ultimately, self-refection is a continuous process. Make it a regular practice in your life, dedicating time to revisit your thoughts and feelings. Journaling can be a helpful tool in this process, providing a space to articulate your reflections and track your progress over time. As you cultivate this habit, you will find that your decision-making skills improve, your confidence grows, and your motivation to engage with the world around you flourishes. By committing to this journey, you empower yourself to make clearer, more compassionate choices that reflect your true values.

The Importance of Awareness

Awareness is the foundation upon which clarity of thought is built. In our daily lives, we often find ourselves swept away by the currents of distractions, emotions, and preconceived notions. This lack of awareness can lead to hasty decisions, increased anxiety, and a sense of being overwhelmed. By cultivating mindfulness, we can develop a heightened awareness that allows us to observe our thoughts and feelings without judgment. This practice not only empowers us to recognize the biases that cloud our judgment but also gives us the tools to navigate challenges with greater confidence and clarity.

Self-awareness is crucial for personal growth and development. It allows individuals to understand their thoughts, emotions, and behaviors, leading to better decision-making. By recognizing their strengths and weaknesses, people can set realistic goals and work towards improvement. Self-awareness fosters emotional intelligence, enhancing relationships through empathy and effective communication. It also enables individuals to manage stress and navigate challenges more effectively, contributing to overall well-being. Moreover, self-awareness promotes authenticity, allowing individuals to align their actions with their values and beliefs, leading to a more fulfilling life.

When we become aware of our thoughts, we gain the ability to distinguish between what is real and what is a product of our biases. Cognitive biases can distort our perceptions, leading us to make choices based on awed reasoning. For instance, we may overlook valuable opportunities because of fear or assume we cannot succeed based on past failures. By practicing mindfulness, we can observe these patterns and understand how they influence our decisions. This awareness enables us to pause, reflect, and choose a more informed response, rather than reacting impulsively.

Mindfulness also fosters a sense of self-compassion, which is crucial for building confidence and motivation. Often, we are our harshest critics, allowing our inner dialogues to undermine our self-esteem and discourage us from pursuing our goals. Through awareness, we can learn to recognize these negative thought patterns and replace them with kinder, more supportive narratives. This shift in perspective not only enhances our self- acceptance but also encourages us to take risks and embrace new challenges, knowing that it's okay to stumble along the way.

Additionally, awareness helps us cultivate an open mindset, allowing us to view situations from various angles. This flexibility is essential when confronting biases that limit our decision-making capabilities. By being mindful, we can actively seek out alternative viewpoints and consider new information without being trapped by our initial reactions. This openness not only enriches our understanding but also fosters healthier relationships with others, as we become more empathetic and willing to listen.

Ultimately, the importance of awareness cannot be overstated. It serves as the gateway to clear thought, better decision-making, and a more fulfilling life. By integrating mindfulness into our daily routines, we can develop the skills needed to overcome biases and make choices that align with our true values and aspirations. Embracing this journey may seem daunting at first, but with consistent practice, we can transform our lives, unlocking the potential to make empowered decisions that lead to personal growth and greater happiness.

Chapter 4: Mindfulness Techniques for Clear Thinking

- Breathing Exercises for Focus
- Meditation to Enhance Clarity
- Mindful Observation in Daily Activities

Breathing Exercises for Focus

Breathing exercises are a powerful tool for enhancing focus and clarity of thought, especially for those who may struggle with decision-making skills, confidence, and motivation. When we feel overwhelmed or distracted, our minds can become cluttered, leading to cognitive biases that cloud our judgment. By incorporating simple breathing techniques into your daily routine, you can create a calming space that allows your thoughts to settle, enabling you to make clearer and more con dent choices.

One of the simplest yet most effective breathing exercises is the 4-7-8 technique. To practice this, find a comfortable seated position and close your eyes. Inhale deeply through your nose for a count of four, hold your breath for a count of seven, and then exhale slowly through your mouth for a count of eight. This exercise not only helps to slow down your heart rate but also shifts your focus away from distracting thoughts. By regularly practicing this technique, you'll find that your ability to concentrate improves, allowing you to tackle decisions with greater clarity and assurance.

Another effective method is the box breathing technique, which is particularly useful when you're feeling anxious or uncertain. Picture a box in your mind as you breathe in: inhale for a count of four, hold for another count of four, exhale for four, and finally hold again for four before starting the cycle anew. This rhythmic pattern can help stabilize your emotions, ensuring that biases stemming from stress or anxiety do not interfere with your decision-making process. As you become more attuned to your breath, you'll cultivate a sense of control over your thoughts and feelings, empowering you to face challenges head-on.

Integrating breathing exercises into your daily life can also enhance your overall mindfulness practice. By taking just a few moments each day to center yourself and focus on your breath, you create a habit of mindfulness that translates into various aspects of your life. This practice fosters a greater awareness of your thoughts and feelings, allowing you to recognize when biases may be influencing your decisions. With continued practice, you'll develop a clearer understanding of your motivations and fears, enabling you to make choices that align more closely with your true values.

In conclusion, breathing exercises serve as a valuable resource for anyone looking to enhance their focus and overcome cognitive biases. By dedicating time to these simple techniques, you not only improve your ability to concentrate but also cultivate a deeper sense of self-awareness. As you become more mindful in your decision-making, you'll notice an increase in confidence and motivation, empowering you to navigate life's choices with greater ease and clarity. Embrace these exercises as your allies on the journey toward a clearer mind and more intentional living.

Meditation to Enhance Clarity

Meditation is a powerful tool that can significantly enhance clarity of thought, allowing individuals to navigate the complexities of decision- making with greater ease. For those who may feel overwhelmed by choices or unsure of their abilities, the practice of meditation offers a refuge. By dedicating just a few minutes each day to this practice, you can cultivate a more focused and open mind. This clarity not only alleviates anxiety but also empowers you to make decisions that align with your true values and goals.

One of the most beneficial aspects of meditation is its ability to help you observe your thoughts without judgment. This practice encourages you to step back from the incessant chatter of your mind and view your thoughts as passing clouds. As you develop this skill, you will begin to notice patterns in your thinking that may have previously gone unnoticed. These insights can illuminate cognitive biases that influence your decision-making, such as confirmation bias or the anchoring effect. Recognizing these biases is the first step toward overcoming them and making more informed choices.

Incorporating mindfulness meditation into your daily routine doesn't have to be complicated. Start by finding a quiet space where you feel comfortable. Sit or lie down, close your eyes, and take a few deep breaths. Focus on your breath as it flows in and out, gently guiding your attention back whenever your mind wanders. This practice not only enhances your ability to concentrate but also cultivates an awareness of your thoughts and feelings.

Over time, you will notice that this heightened awareness spills over into your daily life, enabling you to approach decisions with a clearer, more objective mindset. As you grow more accustomed to meditation, consider applying specific techniques aimed at enhancing clarity. Visualization is a particularly effective strategy. Picture yourself in a situation where you need to make a decision. Imagine the various options and outcomes, allowing yourself to feel the emotions associated with each choice. This mental rehearsal can help you clarify your values and priorities, making it easier to choose a path that resonates with you. The more you practice, the more con dent you will feel in your ability to make decisions that are right for you.

Ultimately, the journey to clarity through meditation is a personal and empowering one. By committing to this practice, you are investing in your ability to think clearly and make choices that reflect who you truly are.

Remember, it's normal to feel uncertain at times, but with consistent effort, you will cultivate a clearer mind and a greater sense of direction. Embrace the process, and trust that each moment spent in meditation is a step toward overcoming the biases that have held you back. With patience and persistence, clarity will become your ally in navigating life's decisions.

Mindful Observation in Daily Activities

Mindful observation in daily activities is a powerful practice that can transform how we approach our thoughts, decisions, and interactions. By engaging in this practice, we cultivate a deeper awareness of our surroundings, our emotions, and the thoughts that arise throughout the day. This heightened sense of awareness allows us to step back from our automatic reactions and biases, giving us the clarity needed to make better choices. It's a gentle reminder that each moment is an opportunity to reconnect with ourselves and to observe the world with fresh eyes.

Incorporating mindful observation into your daily routine doesn't require extensive training or special skills. Start small by dedicating a few moments each day to simply notice what's happening around you. Whether you are sipping your morning coffee, walking to work, or even washing dishes, focus on the sensations and experiences of the moment. Feel the warmth of the cup in your hands, listen to the sounds of your environment, or pay attention to the texture of the soap on your hands. These simple acts of observation can ground you in the present and enhance your mental clarity.

As you practice mindful observation, you will begin to notice the thoughts and judgments that arise. Instead of reacting to these thoughts, try to observe them without judgment. Acknowledge them as they come and go, like clouds drifting across the sky. This practice helps to create a space between your thoughts and your reactions, allowing you to respond more thoughtfully rather than impulsively. Over time, this can significantly reduce the impact of cognitive biases that often cloud our judgment and influence our decisions.

Mindful observation also encourages a sense of curiosity about your experiences. When you approach daily activities with an open mind, you can discover new insights about yourself and your preferences. You may find that certain tasks bring you joy, while others cause stress or frustration. This understanding can empower you to make choices that align more closely with your values and desires. Rather than being driven by external pressures or preconceived notions, you'll be equipped to create a life that feels more authentic and fulfilling.

Ultimately, cultivating the practice of mindful observation can lead to greater confidence and motivation in your decision-making. By developing a clearer understanding of your thoughts, feelings, and biases, you can navigate challenges with a calm and focused mind. Remember, each moment you spend practicing mindfulness is an investment in your ability to make clearer choices and to live a more intentional life. Embrace this journey with an open heart, and allow yourself to grow in awareness and understanding as you move forward.

Chapter 5: Strategies for Overcoming Biases

- Challenging Your Assumptions
- Seeking Diverse Perspectives
- Decision-Making Frameworks

Challenging Your Assumptions

Challenging your assumptions is a vital step towards achieving clarity in thought and making informed decisions. Many of us go through life with a set of beliefs and assumptions that, while comfortable, may not always serve our best interests. These assumptions can cloud our judgment and lead to biases that hinder our ability to make effective choices. By embracing mindfulness, we can create a space to step back, examine these beliefs, and question their validity. This process empowers us to redefine our perspectives and open ourselves to new possibilities.

To begin challenging your assumptions, practice mindfulness techniques that enhance awareness of your thoughts. This can involve simple breathing exercises or focused attention on the present moment. As you cultivate this awareness, pay attention to the beliefs that arise when confronted with a decision. Ask yourself if these beliefs are based on facts or if they stem from past experiences, societal norms, or even fear. Recognizing the origins of your thoughts is an essential first step in dismantling the biases that may be influencing your choices.

Once you have identified these assumptions, it is essential to engage in a process of inquiry. Instead of accepting your initial thoughts as truth, ask yourself probing questions. Why do I believe this? What evidence do I have to support it? What might I be overlooking? This reflective practice not only encourages deeper understanding but also fosters a sense of curiosity. By approaching your beliefs with an open mind, you create room for alternative viewpoints that can lead to more balanced and thoughtful decisions.

In addition to self-inquiry, seeking feedback from others can be a powerful tool in challenging your assumptions. Engaging friends, family, or colleagues in discussions about your perspectives can provide valuable insights. Others may offer viewpoints that you had not considered, helping to reveal blind spots in your thinking. Remember, the goal is not to seek validation but to expand your understanding. Embracing diverse perspectives can significantly enhance your decision-making abilities and boost your confidence in the choices you make.

Ultimately, challenging your assumptions is about reclaiming your power in decision-making. By adopting a mindful approach, you not only clarify your thoughts but also build the confidence necessary to step outside your comfort zone. The journey of self-discovery is ongoing, and it is perfectly natural to encounter doubts along the way. However, with each step taken to question your biases and assumptions, you cultivate a clearer mind and a more empowered self. This newfound clarity will guide you toward making choices that truly align with your values and aspirations, leading to a more fulfilling life.

Seeking Diverse Perspectives

Seeking diverse perspectives is a powerful strategy that can significantly enhance your decision-making capabilities. When faced with choices, it's easy to get trapped in a bubble of familiar thoughts and experiences. Mindfulness encourages you to step back and observe your thoughts without judgment, creating space for curiosity. This practice can help you recognize when you are relying solely on your own viewpoint, which may be limited by your experiences and beliefs. By intentionally seeking out diverse perspectives, you open yourself to a world of ideas that can inform and enrich your decisions.

Engaging with people from different backgrounds can provide insights that you might never have considered. Each person carries a unique set of experiences and knowledge that shapes their viewpoint. By listening to others, you not only gain valuable information but also challenge your own assumptions and biases. This process of exploration can be transformative; it fosters empathy and understanding, allowing you to see issues from multiple angles. As you integrate these varied perspectives, your clarity of thought increases, leading to more well-rounded and informed choices.

Mindfulness plays a crucial role in this journey. When you practice mindfulness, you cultivate an awareness that helps you recognize the moments when you might be dismissing differing opinions too quickly. By grounding yourself in the present, you can approach conversations with an open heart and mind, rather than a defensive stance. This openness encourages genuine dialogue, allowing you to appreciate the richness of conflicting viewpoints. It's important to remember that every perspective has validity, and acknowledging this can create a supportive environment for discussion.

Moreover, actively seeking diverse perspectives can boost your confidence in decision-making. When you know that your choices are informed by a range of opinions and experiences, you can move forward with greater assurance. This collective wisdom helps counteract the fear that often accompanies decision-making, replacing it with a sense of empowerment. The more you practice this approach, the more you develop a habit of considering various viewpoints, making it easier to embrace uncertainty and complexity in your choices.

Ultimately, embracing diverse perspectives is not just a strategy; it's a mindset that fosters growth. As you commit to this practice, you'll find that your ability to navigate life's challenges improves. Each conversation and interaction becomes an opportunity for learning and connection. By harmonizing mindfulness with the pursuit of diverse viewpoints, you will cultivate a clearer mind and make decisions that resonate deeply with your values and goals. Remember, seeking out different perspectives is not just about gathering information; it's about enriching your life and the lives of those around you.

Decision-Making Frameworks

Decision-making frameworks provide structured approaches that can help individuals navigate the often overwhelming process of making choices. These frameworks serve as guides that simplify complex scenarios, allowing you to break down decisions into manageable components. By adopting a decision-making framework, you can enhance your clarity of thought, gain confidence, and reduce the impact of cognitive biases that may cloud your judgment. Embracing these strategies is a step toward taking charge of your choices, fostering a sense of empowerment and control in your life.

One effective decision-making framework is the Rationale-Options- Consequences (ROC) model. This approach encourages you to first identify the rationale behind your decision, which involves understanding your values and goals. Next, you generate a list of possible options, considering both conventional and creative alternatives. Finally, evaluate the potential consequences of each option. By systematically working through these steps, you create a clearer picture of your choices, leading to more informed and con dent decisions. This method not only alleviates anxiety but also helps you recognize the underlying motivations driving your choices.

Incorporating mindfulness into your decision-making process can significantly enhance the effectiveness of these frameworks. Mindfulness encourages you to stay present and fully engaged in the moment, allowing you to observe your thoughts and feelings without judgment. This awareness helps you identify any biases that may influence your decision- making, such as confirmation bias or overconfidence. When you practice mindfulness, you cultivate a sense of calmness that enables you to approach decisions with a clear mind, fostering a more objective evaluation of your options.

Another useful strategy is the Pros and Cons list, which offers a straightforward visual representation of your choices. By listing the advantages and disadvantages of each option, you can see the potential outcomes more clearly. This method encourages you to weigh your options thoughtfully, making it easier to identify the choice that aligns best with your values and objectives. While this technique is simple, it can be incredibly effective in helping you overcome indecision and build confidence in your ability to make sound choices.

Ultimately, adopting decision-making frameworks and integrating mindfulness into your process can transform the way you approach decisions. These strategies empower you to move beyond self-doubt and indecision, allowing you to embrace your capacity for thoughtful, deliberate choices. As you practice using these frameworks, you'll find that your decision-making skills improve, your confidence grows, and you become more adept at navigating the complexities of life. Remember, every small step you take toward enhancing your decision-making abilities is a step toward a clearer mind and a more fulfilling life.

Chapter 6: Building Confidence Through Mindfulness

- The Connection Between Mindfulness and Self-Confidence
- Affirmations and Positive Self-Talk
- Setting Achievable Goals

The Connection Between Mindfulness and Self- Confidence

The practice of mindfulness offers a powerful pathway to enhancing self- confidence. By cultivating present-moment awareness, individuals can develop a clearer understanding of their thoughts and emotions, free from the distractions of judgment and self-doubt. When we learn to observe our minds without getting swept away by negative narratives, we can begin to see ourselves in a more positive light. This shift in perception allows us to acknowledge our strengths and capabilities, gradually building a foundation of self-confidence that empowers us to make better decisions in our lives.

Mindfulness encourages a non-judgmental acceptance of our experiences, which is vital for overcoming cognitive biases that often cloud our judgment. When we are mindful, we can recognize when biases such as fear of failure or perfectionism creep into our thinking. By bringing awareness to these patterns, we can challenge them effectively. For instance, instead of succumbing to the fear of making a wrong choice, mindfulness teaches us to embrace uncertainty and view each decision as an opportunity for growth. This perspective fosters resilience and a willingness to take risks, crucial components of self-confidence.

Moreover, the mindfulness practice of focusing on our breath or bodily sensations anchors us in the present moment. This grounding technique diminishes the overwhelming noise of self-criticism and doubt that can hinder our decision-making abilities. As we become more adept at returning to the present, we can cultivate a sense of inner calm and clarity, which enhances our ability to think critically and make informed choices. As our clarity of thought increases, so too does our self-assurance, enabling us to approach decisions with a greater sense of purpose and conviction.

Engaging in mindfulness also fosters self-compassion, a vital element in building self-confidence. Many people struggle with harsh self-judgment, which can lead to a paralyzing fear of failure. Mindfulness teaches us to treat ourselves with the same kindness and understanding that we would offer a friend. By practicing self-compassion, we can let go of the need for perfection and embrace our imperfections as part of the human experience. This acceptance not only alleviates stress but also empowers us to take action, knowing that mistakes are a natural part of the learning process.

Ultimately, the connection between mindfulness and self-confidence is a transformative journey. By integrating mindfulness into our daily lives, we can break free from the chains of cognitive biases that limit our potential. With each mindful moment, we cultivate greater awareness, self- acceptance, and resilience, paving the way for clearer choices and a more con dent self. As we embark on this journey, we discover that self-confidence is not a destination but a continuous practice, one that unfolds beautifully in the space of awareness and presence.

Affirmations and Positive Self-Talk

Affirmations and positive self-talk are powerful tools that can help reshape your mindset and improve your decision-making skills. When faced with uncertainty or doubt, it is common to fall into negative thought patterns that cloud your judgment. By consciously choosing to replace these negative thoughts with affirmations, you can cultivate a more positive outlook. Start by crafting simple, affirming statements that resonate with you, such as "I am capable of making sound decisions" or "I trust my instincts." Repeating these affirmations regularly can help reinforce a belief in your abilities, leading to greater confidence and clarity in the choices you face.

Integrating affirmations into your daily routine can serve as a reminder of your strengths. Consider starting each day with a few minutes of positive self-talk. Stand in front of a mirror and articulate your affirmations aloud, allowing the words to sink in. This practice not only boosts your self- esteem but also sets a positive tone for the day ahead. Over time, you may notice a shift in your internal dialogue, as your mind begins to replace self- doubt with empowering beliefs. The more you engage with these affirmations, the more natural they will become, helping you to face challenges with renewed confidence.

Another effective strategy is to identify and counteract negative self-talk when it arises. Mindfulness can play a crucial role in this process. By practicing mindfulness, you become more aware of your thoughts and how they influence your feelings and behaviors. When you catch yourself engaging in negative self-talk, pause and take a deep breath. Acknowledge the thought without judgment, then challenge its validity. Ask yourself if the thought is based on facts or assumptions. Often, you will find that the negative thought does not hold up under scrutiny. This awareness allows you to replace it with a more constructive affirmation that aligns with your true capabilities.

In addition to individual affirmations, consider the power of community and shared positivity. Surrounding yourself with supportive individuals who uplift and encourage you can significantly enhance your mindset. Engage in conversations that promote positive self-talk, share affirmations with friends or family, and celebrate each other's successes. This collective positivity can create an environment where confidence flourishes, helping everyone involved to overcome biases and make clearer, more informed decisions. Remember, you are not alone in this journey; support from others can amplify your progress.

Ultimately, the practice of affirmations and positive self-talk is a lifelong journey. As you become more attuned to your thoughts and feelings, you will gradually build a solid foundation of self-assurance and clarity. Embrace the process of self-discovery, and allow yourself the grace to grow. Each small step you take towards nurturing a positive mindset will empower you to make better choices in your life. Trust in your ability to evolve, and remember that every positive affirmation is a step toward a clearer, more con dent you.

Setting Achievable Goals

Setting achievable goals is a crucial step toward enhancing your decision- making skills and building the confidence needed to navigate everyday challenges. When you establish clear, attainable objectives, you create a roadmap that guides your actions and helps you focus on what truly matters. This process can seem daunting, especially if you often feel overwhelmed or lack motivation. However, by breaking down your aspirations into smaller, manageable steps, you can foster a sense of accomplishment and gradually build the momentum needed to make lasting changes in your life.

Begin by identifying what you genuinely want to achieve. Reflect on your values and interests; this self-awareness will serve as a foundation for your goals. Whether it's improving your health, advancing in your career, or enhancing your personal relationships, ensure that your goals resonate with who you are. Mindfulness plays a crucial role here, as it encourages you to stay present and recognize your desires without judgment. Taking the time to sit quietly and contemplate your ambitions can clarify your vision and help you articulate your goals more effectively.

Once you have a clear idea of your aspirations, it's time to break them down into smaller, actionable steps. This approach not only makes you goals less intimidating but also allows you to celebrate small victories along the way. For instance, if your goal is to get t, outline specific actions such as walking for 20 minutes a day or trying a new healthy recipe each week. Each completed step reinforces your commitment and boosts your confidence, making it easier to tackle the next one. Remember, progress is often incremental, and every little achievement counts. As you work on your goals, practice mindfulness to stay focused and present.

Mindfulness can help you overcome cognitive biases that may cloud your judgment and hinder your progress. When faced with setbacks or distractions, take a moment to breathe deeply and center yourself. This practice enables you to respond thoughtfully rather than react impulsively, allowing you to maintain clarity and purpose. By regularly incorporating mindfulness into your routine, you can cultivate resilience and a positive mindset that supports your journey toward achieving your goals.

Lastly, be kind to yourself throughout this process. Understand that everyone encounters obstacles and experiences fluctuations in motivation. Embrace these moments as opportunities for growth rather than signs of failure. By approaching your goals with compassion and patience, you create a nurturing environment that encourages persistence. Celebrate your progress, no matter how small, and remember that every step you take brings you closer to the clarity and confidence you seek. With dedication and mindfulness, you can transform your aspirations into reality and develop the decision-making skills that empower you to lead a fulfilling life.

Chapter 7: Cultivating Motivation

- Mindfulness and Intrinsic Motivation
- Creating a Vision for Your Future
- Overcoming Procrastination with Mindfulness

Mindfulness and Intrinsic Motivation

Mindfulness serves as a powerful tool for enhancing intrinsic motivation, which is the drive that comes from within rather than external rewards. When we practice mindfulness, we cultivate a heightened awareness of our thoughts, feelings, and experiences. This self-awareness allows us to reconnect with our core values and passions, igniting a sense of purpose. For individuals who often feel stuck in their decision-making processes, engaging in mindfulness can clarify what truly matters to them. By regularly reflecting on our motivations and desires, we can foster a more profound understanding of ourselves, which naturally boosts our confidence and willingness to make choices aligned with our true selves.

As we delve into the connection between mindfulness and intrinsic motivation, it is essential to recognize the role of clarity in our thoughts. Mindfulness encourages us to observe our thoughts non-judgmentally, freeing us from the clutter of negative self-talk and cognitive biases that can cloud our judgment. When we take a moment to breathe and ground ourselves in the present, we create a mental space where clarity can flourish. This clarity allows us to sift through the noise and identify what genuinely inspires us. By honing in on our intrinsic motivations, we can make decisions that resonate with our authentic selves, leading to a more fulfilling life.

To harness the benefits of mindfulness and enhance intrinsic motivation, several practical strategies can be employed. One effective approach is to incorporate mindfulness meditation into your daily routine. Even a few minutes of focused breathing or guided meditation can help center your thoughts and foster a deeper connection to your motivations. Journaling is another valuable practice; writing down your thoughts can help clarify your feelings and reveal patterns in your decision-making. By regularly engaging in these activities, you can gradually build a stronger sense of self-awareness, which in turn enhances your intrinsic motivation and decision-making skills.

Moreover, practicing gratitude can significantly impact our intrinsic motivation. When we take time to acknowledge and appreciate the positive aspects of our lives, we shift our focus from what we lack to what we have. This shift in perspective can illuminate our values and desires, making it easier to identify what truly motivates us. Incorporating gratitude exercises into your mindfulness practice can help reinforce a positive mindset, allowing you to approach decisions with a renewed sense of purpose and enthusiasm. By celebrating small victories and recognizing the things that inspire you, you cultivate an environment that nurtures intrinsic motivation.

Lastly, remember that the journey toward enhanced intrinsic motivation through mindfulness is ongoing. It requires patience and commitment, but the rewards are well worth the effort. By consistently practicing mindfulness, you will gradually become more attuned to your inner self, leading to improved decision-making skills and greater confidence. Embrace the process and allow yourself to explore the depths of your motivations. With each mindful moment, you will find clarity of thought and a stronger sense of purpose, empowering you to make choices that reflect your true desires and aspirations.

Creating a Vision for Your Future

Creating a vision for your future is an empowering step that can transform your life. By envisioning where you want to be, you can begin to align your thoughts and actions with that ideal future. It's important to recognize that this vision does not have to be grand or elaborate; it simply needs to resonate with you on a personal level. Start by taking a moment to reflect on your values, passions, and what brings you joy. This reflection will serve as the foundation upon which you can build a clear and motivating vision.

As you begin to craft this vision, consider incorporating mindfulness practices into your daily routine. Mindfulness encourages you to stay present and aware, allowing you to better understand your thoughts and emotions. When you are mindful, you can observe the biases that may cloud your judgment and affect your decision-making. By recognizing these cognitive biases, you can begin to set them aside, creating a clearer mental space where your vision can thrive. This clarity will help you identify the steps necessary to achieve your goals, breaking them down into manageable actions.

Visualizing your future can also enhance your motivation and confidence. Spend time each day imagining yourself living in alignment with your vision. What does your life look like? How do you feel? Engaging your senses in this process can make your vision more tangible and exciting. As you immerse yourself in this mental imagery, you may discover a newfound enthusiasm for taking action. Remember, every small step you take towards your vision is a victory, and acknowledging these achievements can build your confidence over time.

In addition to visualization, writing down your vision can solidify your intentions. Create a vision board or a journal entry that encapsulates your dreams and aspirations. By putting pen to paper, you are not only clarifying your vision but also committing to it. This physical representation of your goals serves as a reminder of what you are working towards, helping you stay focused and motivated. As you encounter challenges or setbacks, revisiting your vision can reignite your passion and remind you of the bigger picture.

Ultimately, creating a vision for your future is about embracing possibilities and fostering a growth mindset. It's a journey that requires patience and self-compassion, allowing you to learn from your experiences along the way. By incorporating mindfulness into this process, you can overcome biases that may have previously held you back. As you cultivate clarity of thought and a sense of purpose, you'll find that your decision-making skills, confidence, and motivation will flourish, guiding you toward the life you envision.

Overcoming Procrastination with Mindfulness

Procrastination is a common challenge faced by many, often rooted in feelings of overwhelm, fear of failure, or perfectionism. These feelings can cloud our judgment and impact our ability to make clear decisions. By incorporating mindfulness into our daily routines, we can break free from the cycle of procrastination. Mindfulness encourages a present-focused mindset, allowing us to acknowledge our thoughts and feelings without judgment. This practice not only helps us understand the underlying reasons for our procrastination but also empowers us to take actionable steps toward our goals.

To effectively combat procrastination with mindfulness, it is essential to cultivate awareness of our thoughts and emotions. When we find ourselves avoiding tasks, we can pause and reflect on what is driving our hesitation. Are we afraid of not meeting expectations? Are we overwhelmed by the size of the task? By naming these feelings, we create space for ourselves to respond thoughtfully rather than react impulsively. This self-awareness helps us gain clarity, allowing us to separate our fears from the actual tasks at hand.

Incorporating mindful practices into our daily lives can also enhance our motivation levels. Simple techniques such as deep breathing or short meditation sessions can ground us in the present moment. These practices reduce anxiety and create a mental environment conducive to productivity. When we take a moment to breathe and focus on the here and now, we can approach our tasks with a clearer mind and renewed energy. This shift in perspective makes it easier to tackle even the most daunting projects, transforming them from sources of stress into manageable challenges.

Another effective strategy for overcoming procrastination is to set small, achievable goals. Mindfulness encourages us to break tasks into bite-sized pieces, making them less intimidating. By focusing on one small step at a time, we can celebrate our progress, no matter how minor it may seem. This practice reinforces a sense of accomplishment and encourages us to keep moving forward. Additionally, staying present and engaged in each step helps us maintain clarity of thought, reducing the likelihood of falling back into old patterns of avoidance.

Finally, embracing a non-judgmental attitude is crucial in overcoming procrastination. Mindfulness teaches us to treat ourselves with kindness and understanding, recognizing that everyone struggles with motivation at times. When we approach our procrastination with compassion rather than criticism, we create a supportive internal dialogue that fosters resilience. Each time we practice this mindset, we reinforce our ability to make clear choices and take decisive action. By integrating mindfulness into our lives, we can not only overcome procrastination but also unlock our full potential for growth and achievement.

Chapter 8: Putting It All Together

- Developing a Personal Mindfulness Routine
- Tracking Your Progress
- Celebrating Your Growth

Developing a Personal Mindfulness Routine

Developing a personal mindfulness routine can significantly enhance your clarity of thought and empower you to make more con dent decisions.

Mindfulness is a simple yet profound practice that encourages you to engage fully with the present moment. By incorporating mindfulness into your daily life, you can cultivate a deeper awareness of your thoughts, feelings, and surroundings, which is crucial for overcoming cognitive biases.

The beauty of mindfulness lies in its accessibility; anyone can start this journey, regardless of their background or experience with meditation.

To create an effective mindfulness routine, begin by identifying a specific time each day when you can dedicate a few moments to yourself. This could be in the morning as you wake up, during your lunch break, or in the evening as you wind down. Consistency is vital, so choose a time that fits your schedule and stick with it. Start with short sessions, perhaps just five minutes, and gradually increase the time as you feel more comfortable. The key is to make this practice a regular part of your life, allowing it to become a reliable tool for fostering clarity and awareness.

In your mindfulness practice, focus on your breath as a means to anchor your attention. Spend a few minutes simply noticing your breath—how it feels as it enters and leaves your body. When your mind wanders, gently bring it back to your breath without judgment. This simple act of returning your focus can help you realize how often your thoughts drift, a common occurrence for many. Over time, this practice enhances your ability to observe your thoughts and emotions, creating a pause that allows for clearer decision-making and reduces the influence of biases that can cloud your judgment.

Incorporating mindfulness into everyday activities can also deepen your practice. Try being fully present during routine tasks, such as eating, walking, or even washing dishes. Notice the sensations, smells, and sounds associated with these experiences. By grounding yourself in the present moment, you train your mind to become more aware and resilient, making it easier to confront biases when they arise. This level of awareness can lead to improved problem-solving skills and a greater sense of control over your decisions.

Finally, remember that developing a mindfulness routine is a personal journey that evolves over time. Be patient with yourself and celebrate your progress, no matter how small. It's completely normal to encounter challenges along the way, but each moment spent practicing mindfulness is a step toward greater clarity and confidence. As you cultivate this routine, you will likely find that your decision-making abilities improve, allowing you to navigate life's complexities with a clearer mind and a more open heart.

Embrace this journey, knowing that the path to overcoming biases and enhancing your choices starts with a single mindful breath.

Tracking Your Progress

Tracking your progress is an essential aspect of harnessing mindfulness to overcome biases and enhance decision-making skills.

By regularly assessing where you stand in your journey, you can cultivate a greater sense of self-awareness and clarity. This practice not only helps you recognize your advancements but also reinforces your commitment to personal growth.

Start by setting clear, achievable goals that align with your values and aspirations. These goals will serve as your benchmarks, allowing you to measure your progress and reflect on the steps you've taken. Incorporating mindfulness into your daily routine can significantly enhance your ability to track progress effectively. Consider dedicating a few moments each day to mindful reflection. This could involve journaling about your thoughts, emotions, and experiences. By writing down your reflections, you create a tangible record of your journey. Over time, this journal will reveal patterns in your thinking and decision-making, providing insights into the biases you may be grappling with. Celebrating small victories along the way will boost your motivation and confidence, reminding you that every step counts.

It's also helpful to create a visual representation of your progress. Whether it's a chart, a vision board, or a simple checklist, seeing your achievements laid out can be incredibly motivating. You might choose to mark off completed tasks or milestones that demonstrate the growth you've achieved. This visual cue serves as a constant reminder of your potential and the positive changes you have made. Keeping your progress visible helps sustain your enthusiasm for the journey ahead, making it easier to stay focused on your goals.

Engaging with a supportive community can further enhance your ability to track progress. Sharing your experiences with others who are on similar paths can provide valuable feedback and encouragement. This connection can help you gain new perspectives and insights into your challenges, making it easier to identify areas for improvement. By discussing your goals and progress with others, you create a network of accountability that fosters growth and encourages you to stay committed to your journey.

Finally, remember that tracking progress is not just about achieving goals; it's also about understanding the process. Embrace the lessons learned from both successes and setbacks. Each experience contributes to your overall growth and clarity of thought. As you navigate through your journey, keep cultivating mindfulness to remain present and aware of your thoughts and feelings. This holistic approach will empower you to overcome cognitive biases, improve your decision-making skills, and ultimately lead you toward a more con dent and fulfilling life.

Celebrating Your Growth

Celebrating your growth is an essential part of the mindfulness journey. As you embark on this path, it is crucial to recognize and appreciate the small victories along the way. Each moment of clarity, every decision made with intention, and every bias acknowledged represents a step forward. By celebrating these milestones, you reinforce your commitment to personal development and create a positive feedback loop that encourages further progress. Remember, growth is not always linear; it is often a series of ups and downs. Embrace each phase, knowing that every experience contributes to your overall journey.

Mindfulness teaches us to observe our thoughts and feelings without judgment. This practice allows you to gain insight into how cognitive biases have influenced your decision-making in the past. As you become more aware, you can celebrate the moments when you recognize these biases, acknowledging the progress you've made in understanding yourself. Each time you notice a bias rather than react to it, you are reclaiming your power.

This awareness is a significant achievement and a testament to your growth. Celebrate these instances, as they mark your evolution from automatic reactions to thoughtful responses. As you become more proficient in mindfulness, you will find that your decisions become clearer and more aligned with your true values. This clarity is an incredible milestone worth celebrating. Take time to reflect on the choices you make and how they differ from those made in the past. Consider how mindfulness has helped you to cut through the noise, allowing you to approach decisions with a clearer mind. Acknowledge the confidence that stems from this clarity. Each decision made with intention is a celebration of your ability to navigate life's complexities with grace and purpose.

Incorporating celebration into your routine can enhance your mindfulness practice. Create rituals that honor your growth, whether it's journaling about your experiences, sharing your insights with a friend, or simply taking a moment to breathe deeply and reflect. These acts of recognition not only reinforce your achievements but also cultivate a sense of joy and gratitude. As you celebrate, you reinforce the positive changes you are making, creating a powerful motivator to continue on your path. Celebrating growth doesn't have to be grand; sometimes, the simplest acknowledgments are the most meaningful.

Finally, as you celebrate your growth, remember that you are not alone on this journey. Many individuals face similar challenges with decision- making, confidence, and motivation. Share your experiences with others, fostering a sense of community and support. By celebrating together, you can inspire and uplift one another. This collective acknowledgment of growth reinforces the idea that transformation is possible for everyone. Embrace your growth, celebrate your journey, and inspire those around you to do the same, knowing that each step forward contributes to a more mindful and intentional life.

Chapter 9: Real-Life Applications

- Mindfulness in Work Decisions
- Navigating Relationships with Clarity
- Making Everyday Choices Mindfully

Mindfulness in Work Decisions

In today's fast-paced world, decision-making can often feel overwhelming. Many individuals find themselves caught in a web of doubts and uncertainties, which can lead to poor choices and missed opportunities. However, cultivating mindfulness can significantly enhance clarity of thought, allowing you to approach decisions with greater confidence and ease. By tuning into the present moment and observing your thoughts without judgment, you can identify the biases that may cloud your judgment and learn to navigate through them effectively.

Mindfulness encourages you to pause before reacting. This pause is crucial when faced with decisions, whether they are as simple as what to eat for lunch or as complex as a career change. By taking a moment to breathe and reflect, you create space to consider your options more clearly. This practice not only helps you to assess the potential outcomes of your decisions but also allows you to connect with your intuition, which often knows what is best for you. When you approach decision-making with a mindful mindset, you're more likely to act in alignment with your values and long-term goals.

Cognitive biases can often skew our perception and lead us to make choices that are not in our best interest. Mindfulness can serve as a powerful tool to recognize these biases as they arise. For instance, confirmation bias might lead you to seek out information that only supports your existing beliefs, while anchoring bias can cause you to rely too heavily on the first piece of information you receive. By practicing mindfulness, you develop the ability to observe these patterns in your thinking. Recognizing when a bias influences your decision allows you to counter it with a more balanced perspective, leading to sounder choices.

To incorporate mindfulness into your decision-making process, consider establishing a simple routine. Begin by setting aside a few minutes each day to practice mindfulness meditation or deep breathing exercises. As you become more familiar with these practices, try applying them when faced with a decision. Ask yourself questions like, "What am I feeling right now?" and "What are the facts of this situation?" This reflection can help you differentiate between emotional responses and rational thoughts, empowering you to make decisions that resonate with your true self.

Embracing mindfulness in your work decisions can lead to profound changes in how you approach challenges and opportunities. By developing a clearer mind, you not only enhance your decision-making skills but also foster a greater sense of confidence and motivation. Remember, every decision is a chance to learn and grow. With practice, you can navigate the complexities of choice with a calm and centered approach, transforming potential obstacles into stepping stones toward your goals.

Navigating Relationships with Clarity

Navigating relationships can feel overwhelming, especially when biases cloud our judgment and emotions take the lead. However, cultivating mindfulness can serve as a guiding light, helping us approach interactions with clarity and intention. By being present in the moment, we can better understand not only our own feelings but also the perspectives of others. This awareness fosters healthier communication and strengthens our connections, allowing us to make decisions that reflect our true values rather than reactive impulses.

To enhance clarity in relationships, it's essential to recognize the cognitive biases that often distort our perceptions. For instance, confirmation bias may lead us to only acknowledge information that aligns with our existing beliefs about others. By practicing mindfulness, we can challenge these biases and open ourselves to a fuller understanding of those we interact with. Taking a step back and observing our thoughts and emotions without judgment enables us to see situations more clearly, paving the way for more balanced and thoughtful responses.

One effective strategy for overcoming these biases is to engage in active listening. When we truly listen to others, we not only validate their feelings but also create a space for genuine dialogue. Mindfulness encourages us to focus on the present moment, allowing us to absorb what the other person is saying without planning our response while they speak. This practice can transform misunderstandings into opportunities for deeper connections, ultimately enhancing our relationships and decision-making processes.

Another powerful tool is the practice of reflection. After conversations or interactions, take a moment to reflect on your thoughts and feelings. Ask yourself questions like, "What assumptions did I make?" or "How did my biases influence my reaction?" This reflective practice fosters self-awareness and helps us identify patterns that may be detrimental to our relationships. Over time, this mindfulness approach can lead to a clearer understanding of ourselves and a more compassionate view of others, enhancing our ability to navigate relationships with confidence.

Ultimately, navigating relationships with clarity is a journey that requires patience and practice. By embracing mindfulness, we can break free from the chains of cognitive biases and foster more authentic connections. Each step toward clarity not only empowers us in our interactions but also enriches our overall experience of life. Remember, it's never too late to cultivate a clearer mind and make choices that resonate with our true selves, leading to more fulfilling relationships.

Making Everyday Choices Mindfully

Making everyday choices mindfully can transform the way we navigate life, especially for those who often feel overwhelmed by decision-making. When faced with a choice, whether it's what to eat for lunch or how to respond to a friend, it's easy to fall into the trap of automatic thinking. By practicing mindfulness, we can cultivate a clearer perspective that allows us to approach each decision with intention and clarity. This shift in mindset empowers us to make choices that align better with our values and needs, ultimately enhancing our overall well-being.

To begin making choices more mindfully, it's essential to pause and take a moment for self-reflection. Before jumping into a decision, ask yourself what truly matters in that moment. This simple act of pausing can help you recognize any biases or preconceived notions that may cloud your judgment. For instance, if you're choosing a meal, consider not just your immediate cravings but also how that meal might affect your energy and mood. This mindful approach encourages a deeper connection to your body and emotions, fostering greater clarity in your decision-making process.

Another effective strategy is to break down your choices into smaller, manageable parts. Instead of feeling overwhelmed by the enormity of a decision, list out the pros and cons of each option. This technique not only clarifies your thoughts but also minimizes the influence of cognitive biases, such as confirmation bias, which can lead you to favor information that supports your initial inclination. By analyzing your choices step by step, you can make more informed decisions that reflect your true desires and priorities.

Incorporating mindfulness into your daily routine can also enhance your confidence in making choices. Consider setting aside a few minutes each day for mindfulness practices such as meditation or deep breathing exercises. These practices help quiet the mind and reduce anxiety, allowing you to approach decisions with a sense of calm and focus. As you build this habit, you'll find that your ability to weigh options and trust your instincts improves significantly, empowering you to make choices that resonate with your authentic self.

Lastly, remember that making choices is a skill that develops over time, and it's perfectly okay to make mistakes along the way. Each decision offers an opportunity for growth and learning. By embracing a mindful approach, you can cultivate resilience in the face of uncertainty, knowing that every choice contributes to your journey. Celebrate your progress, no matter how small, and keep moving forward with the understanding that clarity of thought and mindful decision-making are within your reach.

Chapter 10: Continuing Your Journey

- Resources for Further Learning
- Building a Supportive Community
- Embracing Lifelong Mindfulness

Resources for Further Learning

In your journey toward greater clarity and decision-making skills, a wealth of resources is available to guide and support you. Books, online courses, podcasts, and articles can offer valuable insights and practical strategies to help you cultivate mindfulness and overcome biases. Start by exploring foundational texts on mindfulness, such as "Wherever You Go, There You Are" by Jon Kabat-Zinn. This classic provides simple yet profound teachings on being present, which can significantly enhance your ability to think clearly and make informed decisions.

Online platforms like Coursera and Udemy offer a variety of courses focused on mindfulness and cognitive biases. These courses often feature expert instructors and interactive content that can deepen your understanding and practice. Look for courses that emphasize practical applications, as they can equip you with tools to integrate mindfulness into your daily life. Engaging with structured learning can foster a sense of accomplishment and encourage you to apply what you learn in your decision-making processes.

Podcasts are another fantastic resource for those seeking motivation and inspiration. Shows like "The Mindful Kind" and "Bias Disruption" explore themes related to mindfulness and cognitive biases in an accessible and engaging format. Listening to these discussions can help reinforce your commitment to mindfulness while providing real-life examples of individuals who have transformed their decision-making through mindful practices. This auditory learning can be particularly beneficial for those who may find reading challenging or time-consuming.

In addition to formal resources, consider joining local mindfulness groups or online communities. Connecting with others who share similar goals can provide encouragement and accountability. These groups often offer workshops, meditation sessions, and discussions that can enhance your understanding of mindfulness and its impact on clarity of thought. Sharing experiences with like-minded individuals can boost your confidence and motivation, reminding you that you are not alone on this journey.

Finally, remember that personal reflection is a vital part of your learning process. Keep a journal to track your thoughts, feelings, and decisions as you practice mindfulness. Reflecting on your experiences can help you identify patterns and biases that may influence your choices. This practice not only reinforces your learning but also empowers you to take charge of your decision-making. With dedication and the right resources, you can cultivate a clear mind and make choices that align with your true self.

Building a Supportive Community

Building a supportive community is a crucial step toward fostering clarity of thought and overcoming cognitive biases. Surrounding ourselves with individuals who share similar goals and values can create a nurturing environment where we feel empowered to express ourselves and make informed decisions. When we cultivate relationships with supportive friends, family, or peers, we create a space where our thoughts can be explored and challenged constructively. This exchange of ideas not only promotes personal growth but also enhances our ability to navigate the complexities of decision-making.

In a supportive community, mindfulness plays a vital role in how we connect with others. Practicing mindfulness helps us become more aware of our thoughts and feelings, allowing us to engage more deeply with those around us. By taking the time to listen actively and empathetically to others, we can foster a sense of belonging and acceptance. This environment encourages us to share our struggles and successes, knowing that we are met with understanding rather than judgment. As we practice mindfulness together, we become more adept at recognizing our biases and can challenge them collectively, leading to clearer thinking.

Encouraging open discussions within our community can significantly influence our decision-making skills. When we engage in conversations about our thoughts and the biases that may cloud our judgment, we can identify patterns and triggers that impact our choices. By sharing our experiences and insights, we empower one another to approach decisions with greater awareness. This collaborative process not only builds our confidence but also reinforces the notion that we are not alone in our challenges. The synergy created within a supportive community enhances our capacity to make better, more mindful choices.

To build a supportive community, it is essential to seek out individuals who are committed to personal growth and mindfulness. This can be achieved by participating in local groups, attending workshops, or joining online forums focused on mindfulness and decision-making. As we engage with others on this journey, we can share resources, strategies, and encouragement that help us navigate life's challenges. Finding a community that resonates with our values and aspirations fosters accountability and motivation, driving us to remain committed to our goals.

Ultimately, building a supportive community requires effort and intention, but the rewards are immeasurable. As we surround ourselves with like-minded individuals, we create a network that nurtures our growth and supports our journey toward clarity of thought. Together, we can challenge our biases, enhance our decision-making skills, and cultivate the confidence needed to pursue our aspirations. Embracing this collective journey not only transforms our lives but also empowers us to uplift others, creating a ripple effect of mindfulness and clarity in our communities.

Embracing Lifelong Mindfulness

Embracing lifelong mindfulness is a journey that can transform your everyday decision-making process. Mindfulness invites you to engage fully with the present moment, enhancing your clarity of thought and allowing you to navigate life's challenges with greater confidence and ease. By integrating mindfulness into your daily routine, you cultivate a sense of awareness that empowers you to make more informed choices. As you practice being present, you begin to notice patterns in your thinking and behavior, which helps you recognize when biases creep in and influence your decisions.

To start embracing mindfulness, consider simple strategies that fit seamlessly into your life. Begin with short moments of mindfulness, such as taking a few deep breaths before making a decision. This pause can help ground you and shift your focus from the whirlwind of thoughts to the clarity of the moment. As you develop this habit, you can gradually extend these mindfulness practices to other areas of your life, such as mindful walking or listening. Each practice strengthens your ability to observe your thoughts without judgment, allowing you to differentiate between instinctive reactions and thoughtful responses.

Another powerful aspect of mindfulness is its role in combating cognitive biases. These biases often cloud our judgment and lead to decisions based on emotions or preconceived notions rather than objective analysis. By practicing mindfulness, you create space for reflection and insight. When a bias arises, you can recognize it as just a thought, rather than an absolute truth. This awareness opens the door to more rational thinking, enabling you to evaluate situations more clearly. With time, you will find that your decisions become more aligned with your true values and goals.

Incorporating mindfulness into your life also fosters self-compassion, which is essential for building confidence in decision-making. Rather than criticizing yourself for past choices, mindfulness encourages a gentle acceptance of your experiences. This shift in mindset allows you to learn from mistakes without being weighed down by guilt or self-doubt. As you cultivate self-compassion, you become more willing to take risks and make decisions, knowing that every choice is an opportunity for growth and learning.

Ultimately, embracing lifelong mindfulness is about creating a supportive foundation for your life. It empowers you to face challenges with clarity and confidence while reducing the impact of biases that may have previously held you back. Each mindful moment is a step toward a more intentional life, where you can make choices that reflect your true self. As you embark on this journey, remember that progress takes time, and every small effort contributes to a clearer mind and more fulfilling choices.

As we reach the end of Clear Mind, Clear Choices, it's important to reflect on the journey you've undertaken. Throughout these pages, you've explored the power of mindfulness and its ability to clear the fog of unconscious biases, bringing clarity and intention to your decision-making. You've been introduced to practical tools that enable you to recognize and mitigate the subtle forces shaping your choices, whether in your personal life, professional environments, or interactions with others.

The insights gained are just the beginning. Developing mindfulness is not a one-time effort but an ongoing practice that, with time and dedication, grows deeper and more intuitive. By continuing to nurture self-awareness, you empower yourself to navigate life with greater ease, compassion, and wisdom. The strategies you've learned—from breathing exercises to reflective questioning—are meant to serve as foundational practices, ready to be adapted to your evolving experiences and challenges.

The real work begins now. Integrating these tools into your everyday life is key to sustaining this clarity of mind. Whether it's making small decisions more mindfully or approaching major life choices with renewed focus, you now have the resources to navigate your biases and emotions with greater awareness. In doing so, you not only improve the quality of your own decisions but also contribute to creating a more thoughtful, equitable world around you.

Remember, this journey toward mindful living is not about perfection, but progress. Mistakes will happen, and biases may still arise, but with awareness comes the power to pause, reflect, and choose a different path. Every choice you make mindfully is a step toward personal growth, enhanced relationships, and a clearer, more intentional life.

As you move forward, take the lessons from Clear Mind, Clear Choices with you. Allow mindfulness to guide your decisions, foster deeper connections, and help you embrace each moment with purpose and clarity. This is your journey—a path of self-discovery, growth, and ultimately, transformation.

Thank you for embarking on this journey. May it lead you to not only clearer choices but a clearer mind and a more fulfilling life.